FANTASTIC FACES

TRANSFORM YOURSELF INTO 12 DRAMATIC CHARACTERS

WRITTEN BY HELEN CASEY
PHOTOS BY CAMERON SLATER

National
The...

...OOKS

AUCKLAND

WELCOME TO THE WONDERFUL WORLD OF BEING A THEATRE MAKE-UP ARTIST!

For thousands of years, civilizations around the world have used make-up for beauty, rituals and disguise. From bright red lipstick to scary war paint, make-up has the power to change the way people see us.

In the earliest plays in ancient Greece, performers changed their appearances to help tell stories. In theatres today, a make-up artist works alongside the costume and props team to transform an actor into their character in the play. Sometimes this can be a very small change, such as a set of fake eyelashes and lipstick. Sometimes it can involve hours of careful work, using make-up, prosthetics and fake blood, so the actor looks completely different.

This book gives you an introduction to how we use make-up in the Wigs, Hair and Make-Up department at the National Theatre. Follow the step-by-step instructions to create different looks and use the tips and techniques to design your own scary, hilarious or monstrous creations.

You don't have to be putting on a play to have fun with stage make-up. You could create a look inspired by your favourite book or film character, or a photo or piece of art. Why not start by collecting images for inspiration? And remember to experiment with the make-up designs in this book. Change the colours, make the looks bolder, funnier or more terrifying – and, most importantly, enjoy yourself!

Helen Casey
Deputy Head of Wigs, Hair and Make-Up at the National Theatre

CONTENTS

EXPERT TOP TIPS

Creating a make-up look requires preparation and patience – as well as a steady hand. Here are some top tips for creating your designs.

BEFORE YOU BEGIN

★ Think carefully about what you are trying to achieve with the make-up. Are you going for a bold or subtle look? What colours are you going to use?

★ Sketch your design on paper before you start. It doesn't have to be perfect, but it will help you feel more confident about the direction of your look.

★ Make sure you are clean and well presented. You are working closely with people so don't eat anything smelly or wear strong perfume.

★ Prepare and organize your materials before you start so they are easily to hand. This includes any reference images you might need.

★ Check all your brushes and equipment are clean. Never use dirty tools.

★ Protect your actor's or model's clothing, and tie or clip the hair off the face.

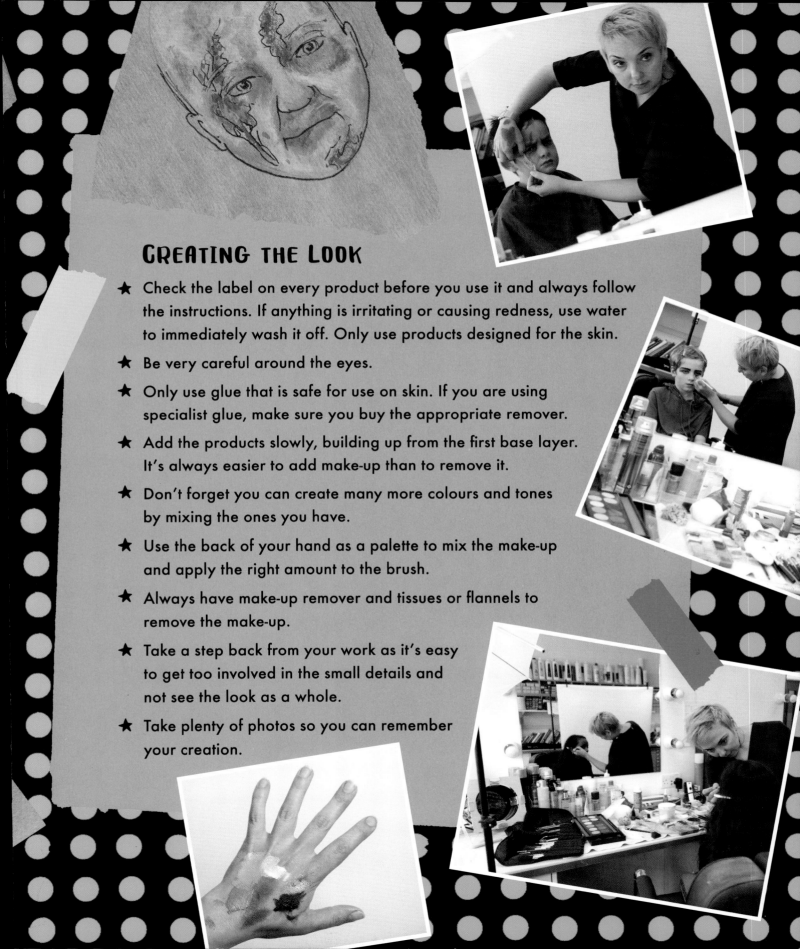

CREATING THE LOOK

★ Check the label on every product before you use it and always follow the instructions. If anything is irritating or causing redness, use water to immediately wash it off. Only use products designed for the skin.

★ Be very careful around the eyes.

★ Only use glue that is safe for use on skin. If you are using specialist glue, make sure you buy the appropriate remover.

★ Add the products slowly, building up from the first base layer. It's always easier to add make-up than to remove it.

★ Don't forget you can create many more colours and tones by mixing the ones you have.

★ Use the back of your hand as a palette to mix the make-up and apply the right amount to the brush.

★ Always have make-up remover and tissues or flannels to remove the make-up.

★ Take a step back from your work as it's easy to get too involved in the small details and not see the look as a whole.

★ Take plenty of photos so you can remember your creation.

INSIDE YOUR MAKE-UP KIT

You will find all these items in a professional theatre make-up artist's kit. They are easy to buy in cosmetic shops, fancy dress shops or online. But don't worry if you haven't got everything on this list – be creative with what you have to hand. It doesn't take much to create dramatic effects.

MAKE-UP PALETTE

The palette should contain the primary colours (red, blue and yellow) as well as green, black and white. It's also useful to have a colour close to your actor's skin tone to use as a base (the first layer of make-up). There are two types of make-up: water-based and grease-paint. They look similar but create different effects.

WATER-BASED MAKE-UP has to be mixed with water and then applied with a brush or sponge. It's easier to use if the water is allowed to soak into the surface of the make-up for a few minutes. It washes off with soap and water – and also sweats off easily. If you've ever had a face-painting kit, this is the kind of make-up you would have used.

GREASE-PAINT is an oil-based make-up. It's applied with a brush or sponge and mixes and blends easily. It needs to be set with powder so it doesn't rub off. It can be taken off with make-up remover.

BRUSHES

★ **POWDER BRUSH:** removing excess powder and applying blusher.

★ **LARGE BRUSH (3-5CM):** applying foundation and large areas of colour.

★ **MEDIUM BRUSH (1-2CM):** applying eyeshadow and blending.

★ **SMALL BRUSH (LESS THAN 1CM):** applying lipstick and drawing details.

SPONGES

Sponges can be natural or latex and are used to apply a variety of textures.

EYESHADOW

Black, brown, white and purple are useful for natural-looking shading. Matt finish is best.

EYE PENCIL AND SHARPENER

Black is essential and other colours will add fun to your looks.

TRANSLUCENT "SETTING" POWDER AND PUFF

Colourless and suitable for all skin tones, this powder is used to set grease-paint to the skin.

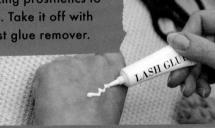

EYELASH GLUE

For sticking prosthetics to the face. Take it off with specialist glue remover.

FAKE BLOOD

Available in many different colours and textures from specialist suppliers. Some are safe to use on clothes. Always check the label.

OTHER USEFUL ITEMS

★ **CAPE OR CLOTHING PROTECTOR**

★ **CLEANSER**

★ **COMB:** useful for all hairstyling.

★ **COTTON BUDS:** good for details and sticking prosthetics to the face.

★ **GLUE REMOVER:** can come as a liquid, cream or gel. Available from specialist suppliers.

★ **HAIR TIES**

★ **MAKE-UP REMOVER**

★ **SPECIALIST THEATRICAL GLUE:** available from specialist suppliers. Requires specialist remover.

★ **TISSUES**

★ **WATER SPRAY:** to mix with your water-based make-up.

SHAPING THE FACE

As a make-up artist, it's very important to know how the bones of the face work together to make it three-dimensional. Stand in front of the mirror and touch your face. Can you feel the bones of your skull under the skin? The shape of your skull defines the shape of your face. Using the actor's bone structure will make the look feel more natural.

SKULL

This skull design is a great way to explore the bone structure of the face. The white highlights the bones under the skin, so try to follow the shape of the skull as closely as possible. The shadows and hollows of the face are emphasized in black, and the teeth complete the look.

KIT LIST

* BLACK EYE PENCIL
* MAKE-UP SPONGE
* WATER-BASED MAKE-UP PALETTE
* MEDIUM AND SMALL BRUSHES
* BLACK EYESHADOW

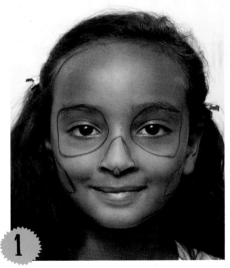

1

Using the eye pencil, draw around the eye sockets, nose and the hollows under the cheek bones.

2

With a sponge, cover the rest of the face, including the lips, with white water-based make-up. You can use a brush for any trickier sections.

3

Once the white is dry, using a medium brush, apply black to the drawn-out areas. Fill in the gap on the tip of the nose with white.

4

Use the small brush to add the teeth: start with a horizontal line through the middle of the lips and then draw vertical lines above and below.

5

Finish the teeth by joining up the vertical lines to create rounded shapes.

6

Use the medium brush and black eyeshadow to add shading around the temples, jaw line and chin. Add black to the neck to make the skull really stand out.

FURTHER LOOKS

★ Add a black hood to complete the character.

★ Swap the black and white around to create a "negative" skull.

★ For an even more shocking look, only paint the skull on one half of the face.

★ Add colourful patterns and a flower crown to create a festival skull.

EXPERT TIP

If you make a mistake, use a cotton bud dipped in make-up remover as an eraser.

OLD WITCH OR WIZARD

Our faces look different depending on the light. Make-up artists often use shading and highlighting to show off different facial features. These techniques are a great way to make an actor look older or younger. Sometimes the look can be as subtle as using a highlighter on the cheekbones or a little shadow under the eye. Or it can be very bold, as with this ageing witch or wizard make-up, which is straight out of a fairy tale.

KIT LIST

* GREASE-PAINT PALETTE
* SMALL AND MEDIUM BRUSHES
* TRANSLUCENT POWDER AND PUFF

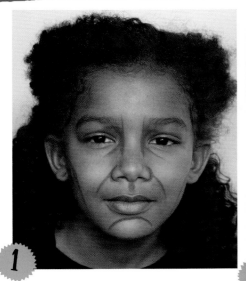

1 Use dark brown grease-paint and the small brush to draw out the areas you want to shade. Make sure the design is symmetrical.

2 Use dark brown and the medium brush to create shadows where you've drawn the outlines. Blend so it is even.

3 Add highlights to the cheeks, forehead, nose and chin: use a lighter colour (try adding some white to a little bit of your brown) and the medium brush. Blend this in too.

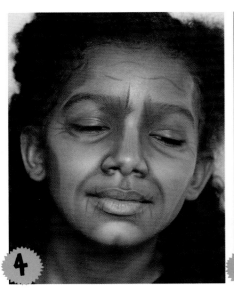

4 Scrunch up the face to find wrinkle points. Use a darker brown and the small brush to draw wrinkles and areas of shadow.

5 Create dramatic eyebrows by exaggerating the natural brows with small flicks.

6 Fix the grease-paint in position by dusting the face with powder.

FURTHER LOOKS

★ Transform this look into a terrifying troll by using a green base.

★ Find a photo of an older relative. Use shading and highlighting to make yourself look like them.

★ Use a toothbrush to comb white water-based make-up through the hair to create grey hair.

EXPERT TIP
Create warts by scrunching up tissue paper and sticking on with eyelash glue.

When creating a make-up look for an actor, it's important to consider the period in history, the society and culture that the character comes from. What is considered beautiful will change depending on the time or place. Make-up artists research the world of the story so the look of the character is as true to life as possible.

ANCIENT EGYPTIAN PHARAOH

Make-up was very important to the ancient Egyptians, who lived thousands of years ago. Kings and queens, known as pharaohs, even had their make-up buried with them. Both men and women wore heavy black and turquoise eye make-up, which they believed protected them from the sun and warded off evil spirits. Try this powerful look which emphasizes the eyes.

KIT LIST

* BLACK EYE PENCIL
* GREASE-PAINT PALETTE
* SMALL AND MEDIUM BRUSHES
* TRANSLUCENT POWDER AND PUFF
* GOLD MAKE-UP OR EYESHADOW

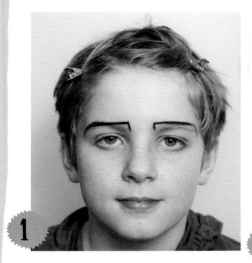

1

Using the eye pencil or black grease-paint and a small brush, draw a straight line just above each eyebrow and extend out beyond it.

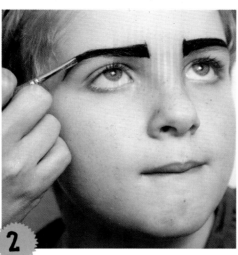

2

Taking this line as the top, use the small brush to draw a bold eyebrow shape. Fill it in with black.

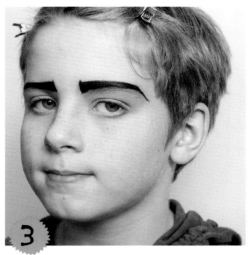

3

Use green and blue to mix a turquoise colour. Apply using a medium brush over the eyelids, right up to the new eyebrows. Powder to fix.

4

Using the black eye pencil or small brush, draw a thick black line around the eye and extend out into a small triangle.

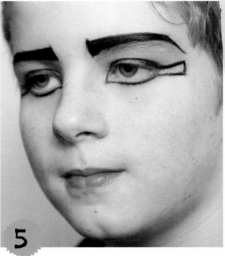

5

Fill in the triangle with gold using the small brush.

6

Using the eye pencil, carefully draw the shape of the Eye of Horus (a powerful Egyptian symbol) under one eye.

FURTHER LOOKS

★ Finish the Egyptian look by adding a wig made of wool, or a card headdress.

★ Use a gold base on the face to turn this look into the mask of Tutankhamun.

★ Use a silver base to transform the look into an ice king or queen. Create your own magical symbol and use glitter to decorate.

EXPERT TIP
When applying eyeliner, always paint under the eye first. This will help avoid smudging.

ROCK STAR

The 1960s and 70s were the era of rock music. Musicians such as David Bowie and Siouxsie Sioux were as famous for their iconic stage looks as they were for their music. Their dramatic make-up was inspired by art from other cultures, and was very different to what was considered beautiful at the time. But their bold looks, which were neither masculine nor feminine, created an entirely new idea of beauty and glamour. Use bright colours and interesting shapes for this rock star look.

* WATER-BASED MAKE-UP PALETTE
* SMALL AND MEDIUM BRUSHES
* EYESHADOW
* COTTON BUD
* VASELINE
* ECO-FRIENDLY GLITTER OR METALLIC COLOURS

1

Using a small brush and a bright water-based colour, draw a lightning bolt which comes down the face and over the eye.

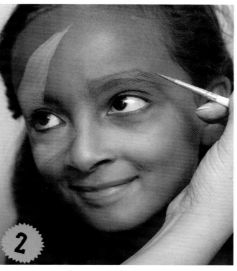

2

Use a small brush and a contrasting colour to draw over and extend the opposite eyebrow.

3

With a matching eyeshadow and a medium brush, fill in the eyelid up to the eyebrow.

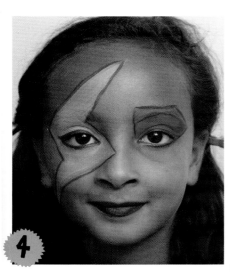

4

To make the shapes stand out, use the small brush to outline them in black. Paint the lips black to be really rock 'n' roll.

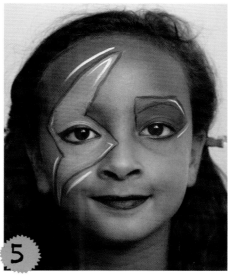

5

Add highlights to the lightning bolt and eye shape using a small brush and white.

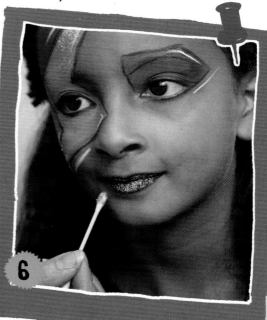

6

Using a cotton bud, apply Vaseline to the ends of the lightning bolt and the lips. Dip the cotton bud in glitter and dab on to the Vaseline.

FURTHER LOOKS

★ Embellish this look by adding squares and triangles with eyeliner. You can also cut out a piece of card as a stencil to make interesting shapes with eyeshadow.

★ Don't forget the hair! You want your whole look to feel glamorous. Slick it down with gel or backcomb with hairspray.

★ For a Siouxsie Sioux goth look, smudge eyeliner under the eye and use a pale base foundation.

EXPERT TIP
Use your hand as a palette to mix and apply colours.

ANIMALS AND MONSTERS

Make-up artists can completely change the shape or look of an actor's face using fake body parts called prosthetics. They can be as small as a wart or as noticeable as a new nose. They are also a great way to create animals, monsters and imaginary creatures.

SEA MONSTER

Prosthetics can take ages to apply and be very hot and uncomfortable to wear. Make-up artists have to ensure the performer is comfortable during the application and then onstage. For full-body prosthetics on a film set, a team of make-up artists can be working up to eight hours to get the actor ready. Don't worry, this scaly sea monster won't take that long, but it will give you a good idea of the process.

KIT LIST

* THICK PAPER
* SCISSORS
* POSTER PAINT
* WATER-BASED MAKE-UP PALETTE
* SMALL AND MEDIUM BRUSHES
* FRUIT BAG OR NETTING
* MAKE-UP SPONGE
* COTTON BUD
* EYELASH GLUE

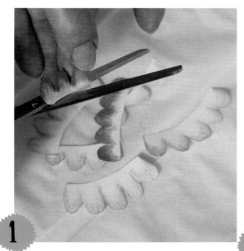

1 Use blue poster paint or make-up to paint scales on thick paper. Carefully cut them out in clusters.

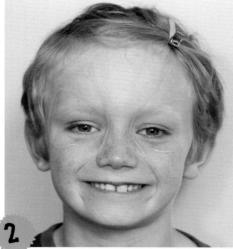

2 Using a small brush and a mid-blue water-based colour, mark out a Y shape from the forehead around the nose. Draw half circles around the eyes and a U shape on the chin.

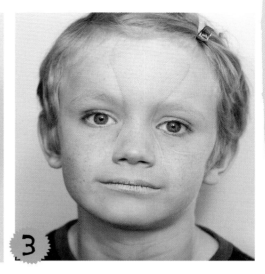

3 With the medium brush, fill in these areas with the mid-blue colour.

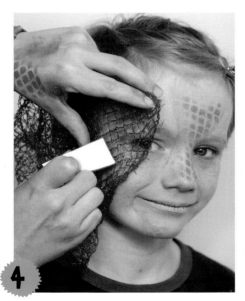

4 Use a sponge and a dark blue colour to dab through the fruit bag to create the texture of scales.

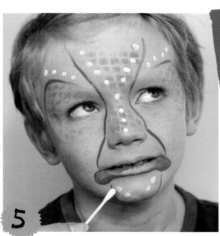

5 Outline the edges of the shapes with a small brush and dark blue. Draw in a big lower lip. Add white spots with a cotton bud.

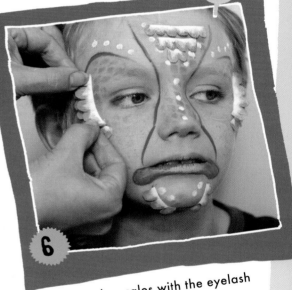

6 Glue on the scales with the eyelash glue. Shape them to the design.

FURTHER LOOKS

★ Use warm tones and triangular scales to transform this design into a dragon.

★ To make an alien, use circular scales and grey tones.

★ To create a mermaid or a merman, paint the scales around the eyebrows and around the hairline. Choose a lip colour that matches the scales.

EXPERT TIP
Lay out all your prosthetics and make-up before you start. It's easy to forget something when you are concentrating on your work.

* CARD
* SCISSORS
* POSTER PAINT (OPTIONAL)
* CRAFT FEATHERS (OPTIONAL)
* WATER-BASED MAKE-UP PALETTE
* MEDIUM AND SMALL BRUSHES
* TEXTURE SPONGE
* EYELASH GLUE

PHOENIX

Make-up artists can use prosthetics to turn an actor into an animal or bird by creating fur or feather effects. The phoenix is a bird from ancient Greek mythology that is reborn through fire. This make-up look brings together feathers and flames to tell the phoenix's story.

ANIMALS AND MONSTERS

1. Cut out feathers and flame shapes from the card. Use paint or make-up to colour them in orange, yellow and red. You can use craft feathers too.

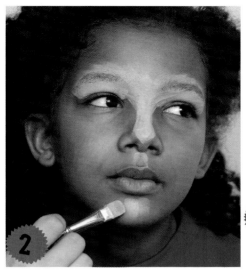

2. Using a medium brush, apply a water-based yellow colour over the eyelids, eyebrows, nose and under the chin.

3. With a texture sponge, add orange around the edges of the yellow on the forehead. Use a small brush to draw orange lines under the eyes and a flame shape in the middle of the forehead.

4. Once dry, using a small brush, draw black lines around the eyes and down the sides of the nose. Outline the flame in black.

5. Use a small brush to add lines of black, white and orange around the face. Line the top lip in black.

6. Stick on your feathers and flames using eyelash glue.

FURTHER LOOKS

★ Cut out leaf shapes and use woodland colours to turn into an elf or pixie.

★ Use grey, black and fake blood to create a fierce werewolf.

★ For a tropical bird or butterfly, use bright colours and paper feathers or antennae around the eye sockets.

EXPERT TIP
Cut up sponges to create texture stamps that look like animal fur, scales or feathers.

Make-up doesn't just have to be about making an actor stand out. It can also be used as a disguise or to create optical illusions that trick the eye.

SOLDIER

Over millions of years, animals have evolved camouflage markings to protect them from predators. Make-up artists copy this effect by breaking up the normal patterns of light and shade on the face. Have a go at blending into the background by creating this soldier camouflage.

KIT LIST

- GREASE-PAINT PALETTE
- SMALL AND LARGE BRUSHES
- TRANSLUCENT POWDER AND PUFF

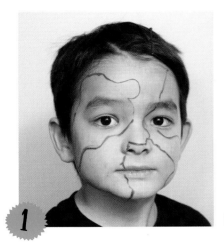

1
Use a small brush and brown grease-paint to mark out the areas of the face you are going to shade light, mid and dark.

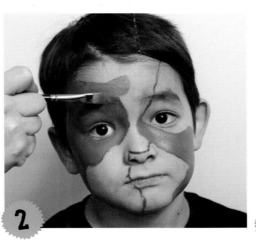

2
Use khaki green and the large brush to fill in the area you've marked out around one eye. Then paint the space on the opposite cheek.

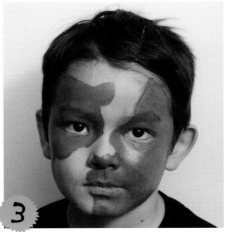

3
Use brown to paint the middle section over the mouth and bottom of the nose. Then paint the section over the other eye.

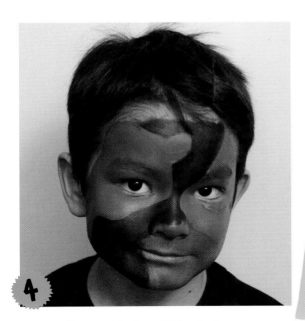

4
Finally, use black to fill in the last sections along the forehead, top of the nose and down the other cheek.

5
Powder to fix the grease-paint and reduce shine.

FURTHER LOOKS

★ For desert camouflage, use a pale sandy colour and a mid and dark brown.

★ For city camouflage, use grey, brown and black.

★ You can use the same effects to become an animal. Try black and white for a zebra or orange and brown for a tiger.

EXPERT TIP
It's easier to cover a light area with a dark colour, so always use your light make-up first and work towards the darkest shade.

Stone Statue

Make-up artists usually focus on the face. But body painters use the entire body to create effects. There are lots of different methods to trick the eye and create visual illusions. These include making skin look like metal, marble or wood. In art this technique is called by the French name, *trompe l'œil*. When you are trying to make an actor look like something else, make sure you have lots of reference images and carefully copy the original colours and shapes. Have a go at this stone statue head – if you feel brave, try the whole body.

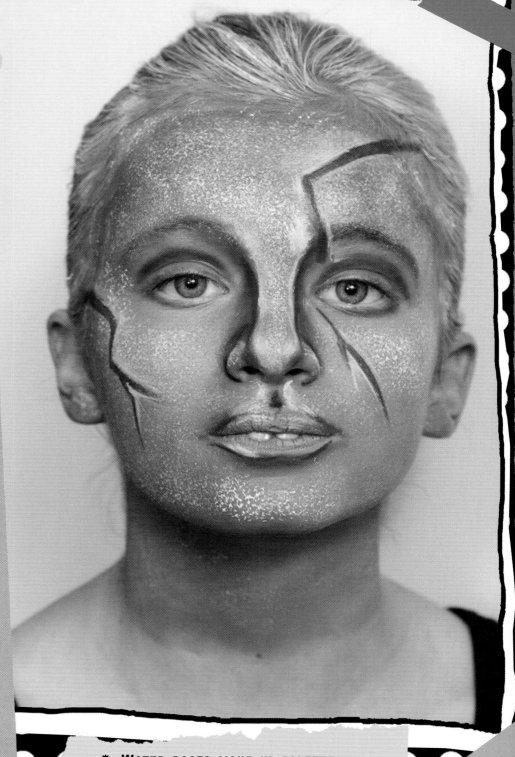

KIT LIST

* **Water-based make-up palette**
* **Large, medium and small brushes**
* **Black eyeshadow**
* **Texture sponge**
* **Black eye pencil**

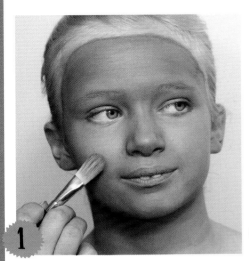

1 Apply a grey water-based colour all over the face, neck and ears using a large brush.

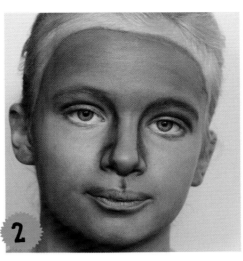

2 Using the black eyeshadow and a medium brush, add shading along the sides of the nose, around the eye sockets, lips and under the chin.

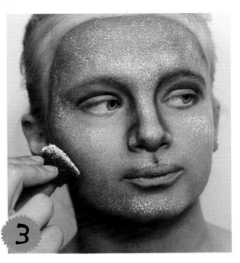

3 Use the texture sponge to apply mid-grey and white all over the face. Don't make it too even so it has an interesting texture.

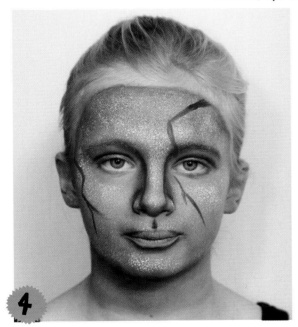

4 Using an eye pencil, draw on thin black cracks zig-zagging across the face. Outline the lips.

5 Using the small brush and pale grey, highlight the cracks, the edges of the nose, the lips and the area under the nose.

FURTHER LOOKS

★ Add some green textures and stick on some fake moss and ivy leaves to make the statue look overgrown.

★ Use a brown base and a wood texture to turn your statue into a wood carving.

★ Use blue and green make-up with red and brown texture to make a bronze statue that has been under the sea.

EXPERT TIP
Extend the colour to the hair line and comb it through the hair using a toothbrush.

BLOOD AND BRUISES

Casualty special effects, such as cuts and bruises, are a large part of the job for any make-up artist. These make-up looks often tell a big part of the story, so it's very important that they seem as real as possible.

PIRATE

If you are creating a cut, scar, bruise or injury, think about what has happened to the character. Have they just been injured, or did it happen the day before? Have they been to the hospital or had first aid? All these things will change how you approach the make-up. You could look at medical reference images to help make the design accurate. Start with this pirate, who has just been wounded in a fierce battle.

KIT LIST

* GREASE-PAINT PALETTE
* TEXTURE SPONGE
* SMALL BRUSH
* BLACK AND GREY EYESHADOW
* WATER-BASED MAKE-UP PALETTE
* FAKE BLOOD
* TRANSLUCENT POWDER AND PUFF

1

Create a bruise by blending in a little yellow and green grease-paint with a texture sponge. Then add purple and dark blue.

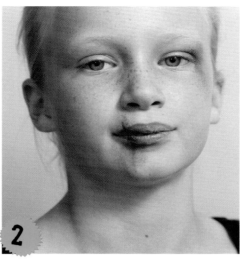

2

Use the sponge and red grease-paint to create an injury area over the lip. Use a small brush and darker red to draw the cut.

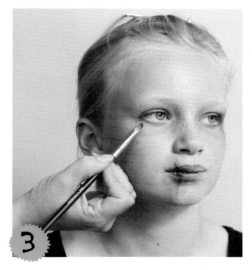

3

Use a little grey eyeshadow for circles around the eyes. Add black eyeshadow under the eyeline.

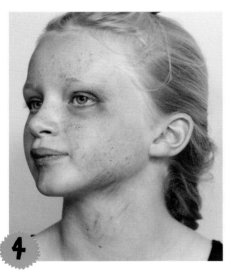

4

Use light brown water-based make-up and the sponge to add some dirt patches on the cheeks and neck.

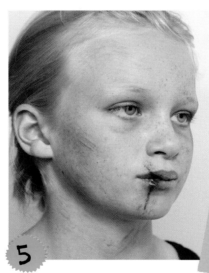

5

Apply fake blood with the small brush to the lip cut, and with the texture sponge over the top of the bruise.

6

Powder the face to fix the make-up.

FURTHER LOOKS

★ Use eyelash glue to stick some small stitches made from knots of black cotton on the cuts. Alternatively, cut up strips of medical tape.

★ Crush up some rice puffs breakfast cereal, mix in a little fake blood and eyelash glue and use the mixture to make scabs.

EXPERT TIP
Don't be too neat with your cuts and bruises. If a bruise is a perfect circle, it will look fake.

ZOMBIE

Zombies are always fun for make-up artists because they are so imaginative. They can be realistic, funny, weird or scary. Whatever you decide, the make-up should tell the story of your zombie. Zombies are the walking dead, so pale textured skin and sunken eyes are always good places to begin. You can add all sorts of cuts, scars and injuries to your finished look.

BLOOD AND BRUISES

KIT LIST

* TISSUES
* NON-TOXIC PVA GLUE
* GREASE-PAINT PALETTE
* MEDIUM AND SMALL BRUSHES
* MAKE-UP SPONGE
* WATER-BASED MAKE-UP PALETTE
* TRANSLUCENT POWDER AND PUFF
* EYELASH GLUE
* COTTON BUD
* FAKE BLOOD

1

Create pieces of skin using single layer tissues and a mixture of 50:50 PVA glue and water. Mix them together on a non-stick surface like a plate. Paint them with a mix of grey and khaki green grease-paint.

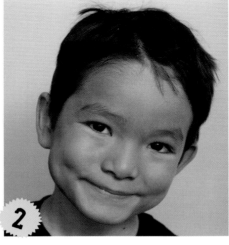

2

Use the medium brush to cover the entire face in a mix of grey and khaki green. Blend with a sponge. Don't make it too even.

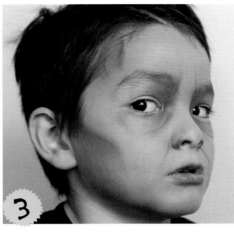

3

With a medium brush and a darker brown or grey, add areas of shadow under the eyes and chin, in the hollows of the cheeks and the sides of the nose and forehead. Blend.

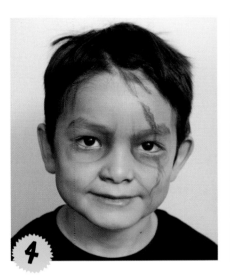

4

Use a small brush to add a water-based red under the eyes and on the eyelids. Paint a cut across one eye.

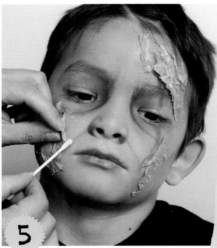

5

Set the base with powder. Stick on the tissue pieces with eyelash glue, using a cotton bud to help you apply them.

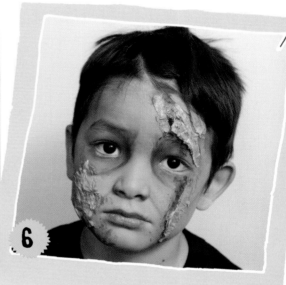

6

Use a small brush to apply fake blood along the cut. Dab on to the tissue paper skin and the chin.

FURTHER LOOKS

★ Transform this zombie into a mummy by using brown make-up tones and black lips. Use some old strips of cloth for mummy bandages.

★ Stick on shells and seaweed cut from green tissue paper to make this a pirate zombie.

★ Add bloody teeth and pointy eyebrows to turn this look into a vampire.

EXPERT TIP
When preparing your zombie skin, experiment with different kinds of tissue paper and thin material to create interesting textures.

An actor's look tells the audience a lot about their character: their job, their home life and their role in the story. Make-up is an important part of this, and the way it has been used in theatres has changed with history.

EVIL GENIUS

In Victorian times, actors used heavy make-up to help the audience see their faces under bright stage lights. They would also exaggerate certain features to reveal aspects of their character to the audience. You can use Victorian make-up techniques to transform yourself into an ultimate baddie. Here the sunken cheeks, shadowy eyes and arched eyebrows of this make-up design suggest the character is suspicious, while the moustache makes him look vain and even a little silly!

KIT LIST

* BLACK EYE PENCIL
* PURPLE, DARK GREY AND GREY EYESHADOW (OR GREASE-PAINT PALETTE)
* SMALL BRUSH
* TRANSLUCENT POWDER AND PUFF (IF USING GREASE-PAINT)

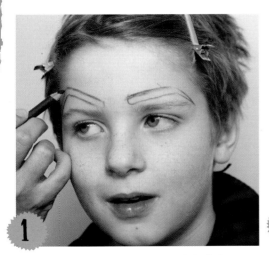

1

Using a black eye pencil, lightly draw out the arched eyebrows with a thin line. Draw them above the real eyebrows.

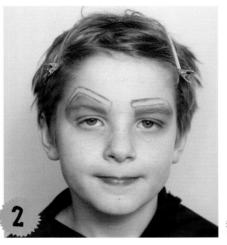

2

With a small brush, apply purple eyeshadow over the eyelids, all the way up to the false eyebrows. Add a little underneath the eyes.

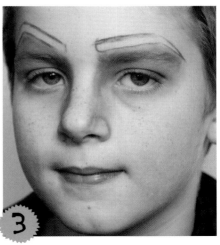

3

Use dark grey eyeshadow lightly on the lower lid, and bring it down the sides of the nose to make it look pointy.

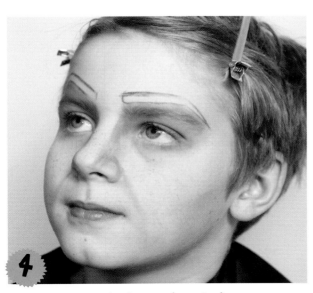

4

Use grey eyeshadow to draw in the nose-to-mouth lines and shade under the cheekbones and on the chin. If you're using grease-paint, fix it with powder.

5

Use the eye pencil to draw in the eyebrows. Add evil scowl lines at the inner edge of each eyebrow. Then draw a dark line just underneath the lower eyelid. Finally, draw a moustache.

FURTHER LOOKS

★ For a circus strongman, add rosy cheeks and a stripy vest top.

★ For a wicked queen, use a white base with the same eyes and face as the villain. Add pointy, pursed lips.

★ Look at your favourite book or cartoon character. Think about how you could use make-up to capture the exaggerated features of their character.

EXPERT TIP
Always sharpen your eye pencil before you use it, especially when you are drawing fine lines.

CLOWN

Clowns are one of the most recognizable types of performers. Clowning has been popular for thousands of years, but it was Joseph Grimaldi in the eighteenth century who began using make-up to bring his clown to life. Clowns now have their own individual make-up looks which they design themselves. The make-up tells a story about the personality of the clown and helps to animate their face. Lots of clowns are silly and clumsy, some are sad, others are sweet and friendly. Try experimenting by painting yourself in different clown faces and see how it makes you feel.

CREATING CHARACTER

KIT LIST

* WATER-BASED MAKE-UP PALETTE
* SMALL, MEDIUM AND LARGE BRUSHES

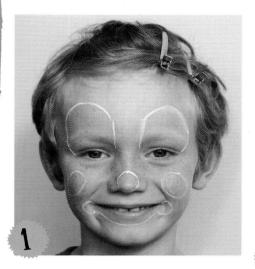

1

Using a small brush and white water-based make-up, draw the outlines of the clown's mouth, eyebrows, and cheek and nose shapes.

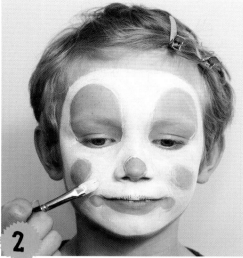

2

Using the large brush, fill in the other areas of the face white.

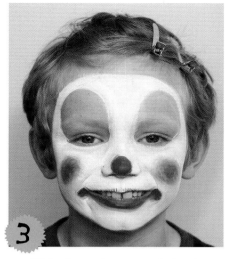

3

Fill in the red nose and cheeks using a small brush.

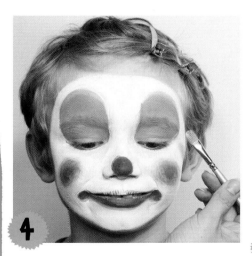

4

Using a medium brush, paint the eyelids a bold colour. Take the colour above your natural eyebrows. Leave a gap between the top of the shape and the white.

5

Using a medium brush and black, fill in the eyebrow shape. They can be thin or fat, smooth or wiggly.

6

Outline the shapes in black using a small brush. Draw black lines down the centre of the eyelids.

FURTHER LOOKS

★ Try different shaped eyebrows. Down at the outer corners will make a sad clown, down at the inner corners an angry one.

★ Draw eyelashes under the eyes to make the eyes look extra large.

★ Try a huge mouth turned up at the corners or a tiny little mouth turned down at the corners. How do these changes affect your performance?

EXPERT TIP
Combine with other techniques in this book (such as ageing or bruises) to make your character's make-up really interesting.

WITH THANKS TO:

ALISA AUCHAYBUR
JOJO GALLAGHER
AMBER-ROSE GIRMAY
FELIX SCLATER
FREYA SCLATER
DAIKI VERNON

All activities are for informational and/or entertainment purposes only, and if in doubt, adult supervision should be required. Walker Books Ltd cannot be held responsible for any injuries which may occur as a result of these activities.

First published 2019 by Walker Books Ltd
87 Vauxhall Walk, London SE11 5HJ

1 2 3 4 5 6 7 8 9 10

Written by Helen Casey

Photos by Cameron Slater

Copyright © 2019 Royal National Theatre

The right of the Royal National Theatre to be identified as the author of this work has been asserted by them in accordance with the Copyright, Designs and Patents Act 1988

This book has been typeset in Futura, WB Fantastic and Leah Gaviota

Printed in China

British Library Cataloguing in Publication Data:
a catalogue record for this book is available from the British Library

ISBN 978-1-4063-8415-4

www.walker.co.uk
www.nationaltheatre.org.uk